GRANDMA'S KITCHEN

Recipes from Slovenia

*The recipes belong to Slovenian traditional cuisine
that is revived by Slovenian primary school pupils.*

Ljubljana, 2019

CIP - Kataložni zapis o publikaciji
Narodna in univerzitetna knjižnica, Ljubljana

641.56(497.4)(083.12)

GRANDMA'S kitchen : recipes from Slovenia / [editors Anka Peljhan and Polona Prešeren ; text about regions Tanja Glogovčan ; photos Igor Zaplatil and Ljubo Vukelić ; translation Secretariat-General of the Government of the Republic of Slovenia, Translation and Interpretation Division, DZTPS, Amidas]. - 3rd reprint. - Ljubljana : Government Communication Office of the Republic of Slovenia, 2019

ISBN 978-961-6435-60-4
1. Peljhan, Anka
COBISS.SI-ID 299536896

CONTENT

FOREWORD BY ANKA PELJHAN   5

FOREWORD BY DR JANEZ BOGATAJ   6

LJUBLJANA AND THE SURROUNDING AREA   10

DOLENJSKA, BELA KRAJINA AND KOČEVSKA   28

POSAVJE AND ZASAVJE   40

KOZJANSKO AND BIZELJSKO   52

PODRAVJE   62

PREKMURJE AND PRLEKIJA   76

UPPER AND LOWER SAVINJA VALLEY, ŠALEK VALLEY   88

KOROŠKA   100

GORENJSKA   112

THE SOČA VALLEY, GORIŠKA BRDA, VIPAVA VALLEY   126

NOTRANJSKA, KARST, ISTRIA   144

LETTER FROM ANA ROŠ   158

KUHNAPATO PROJECT

Children from Slovenian primary schools have ventured where experts rarely take a peek – into the kitchens of their grandmothers, relatives and neighbours. Through the *Kuhnapato* research project, which involves beneficial trans-generational communication, they are treating us with almost forgotten dishes that have left a significant mark in the specific cultures of certain places, towns and villages. Throughout this project and through collaboration with renowned chefs, the kids gain a tremendous cooking experience and enthusiasm while creating dishes that are worthy of becoming gastronomical trademarks of their regions and an additional reason for tourists to visit them.

Such simple dishes, which combine some rare local and seasonal ingredients typical of specific geographical areas, have an appealing and authentic taste which gives us the confidence to consider Slovenian culinary achievements as great as those of the famous culinary superpowers. From its humble beginnings, the project has evolved into a movement with specific goals, such as encouraging youth to respect their own culinary heritage, learning about and using locally grown food in modern cooking, and motivating them to broaden their knowledge about the geographical and cultural origins of local dishes. Through cooperation between primary school pupils, their teachers, caregivers and experts, this project connects the whole Slovenian public.

With their ever growing desire for participation in this project, these kids convinced us that the vaults of our culinary heritage have not been emptied yet. Therefore we bow with respect to all these creative cooks, researchers and food producers for taking the path of responsibility and proving that they really do care! This path they have chosen leads to long-term health benefits, preservation of farms and related jobs, and it nurtures respect and understanding for one's surroundings through research of local cultural history and local seasonal and geographical peculiarities. It is the path of learning about superb culinary achievements and creations and sophisticated flavours, the path of education and preservation of one's own nation! In order to build a firm base for our future, we need to learn about our history – including the history of our food.

During the past six years of research, Slovenian primary school pupils have saved from fading into oblivion more than 1000 dishes, related cooking techniques and the cultural background, all of which were published in five cookbooks. This cookbook contains a selection of interesting and tasty regional dishes which were presented by children and have gained most accolades from culinary experts and sophisticated gourmets. We wish you a pleasant read and *bon appétit*!

Anka Peljhan, Project Manager

Children discover the wealth of local and regional flavours in Slovenia

The activity called *Kuhnapato* (Cooking and all that), or exploring the cultural heritage of food, which is organised each year by Slovenian primary schools and is the basis for the dishes presented here, can be seen as a great success and as something educationally important.

The main purpose of this project is to motivate children in nine-year primary schools to get to know the features of their local and regional food and the characteristics of their cultural environments. The project's aim is therefore focused on the cultural heritage of food, but not in some romantic, museum-style approach but as an understanding of the causal relationships between certain dishes and parallel economic, social and spiritual efforts in certain periods and social milieux.

The project leadership seeks as far as possible each year to ensure that children enter these culinary worlds as independently as possible, in other words in ways appropriate to their knowledge, abilities and world. In this the mentors guide them, but never to an extent that would compromise the authenticity of their grasp and culinary knowledge.

At the IGCAT (Institute for Gastronomy, Culture, Art and Tourism) conference in Barcelona in 2015, a presentation drew considerable attention to the Slovenian school project, and a whole range of European countries today are trying to transfer the wealth of culinary experience to younger generations, which is one of the strongest guarantees for preserving and creatively building on the culinary character of individual local and regional environments or even food cultures.

For this reason it is with nothing but pleasure that I welcome the intention of the Slovenian Government Communication Office to take a selection of dishes, which have been chosen and cooked by children in the six years of the project, and present them in this publication. This is the work of children supported by the knowledge of their forebears or through intergenerational communication, and reflects their ability to understand the cultural heritage of food in their own cultural environment. It is especially pleasing that this involves different age groups of children from nine-year primary schools.

Indeed any efforts in this field must be aimed precisely at young people of primary school age. We must enable them to show their perspective in discovering everything that we label as positive in human nutrition. This includes respect for sustainable food that is close to nature, seasonal food and dishes and seeking out new forms of nutrition using the rich traditions of our food heritage. The Kuhnapato project is therefore much more than just one of the multiple actions or assignments in the Slovenian education system.

The beginning and development of this project is not in fact a coincidence, for ever since 2006 Slovenia has had a Gastronomic Strategy that directs some of its measures to the area of education. Slovenia is divided into 24 gastronomic regions characterised by a total of 315 typical or prominent dishes. In a relatively small geographical area, over the centuries we have seen the development of a range of food diversity, which brings together the influences of the Alps, the Mediterranean and the Pannonian area, and since the end of the Second World War the neighbouring Balkans. Yet we must understand this food diversity above all as an inexhaustible source of creating new dishes, meals and eating habits, including methods of preparation. Moreover, each dish is tied to one or another story from history that can lead us to what an old Slovenian saying tells us: We eat to live, but we don't live just to eat.

The book now in front of you has therefore been "cooked up" by primary school children. Many dishes that have even been forgotten are being prepared again in quite a few families, thanks to the children, and this allows people to sample flavours that have often been removed from nature and people's everyday lives and special days. May our Slovenian experience therefore be an inspiration to others around the world.

Dr Janez Bogataj

CUISINE – A FEW GENERAL WORDS ABOUT SLOVENIAN COOKING

In Slovenia, the way to a person's heart is through their stomach. Food has an extremely important power in identifying Slovenia and its history. In terms of gastronomy, Slovenia offers a colourful image of diversity. What makes it special is its location at the meeting point of the Alps, the Mediterranean and the Pannonian Plain.

Slovenian cuisine is traditionally based on grains, dairy products, meat (especially pork), sea and freshwater fish, vegetables, legumes and tubers, olives and grapes. It is enriched with fine wines and other alcoholic beverages. Several dishes and food products are protected under the uniform regulations of the European Union. It should also be pointed out that throughout Slovenia water is drinkable and of excellent quality. There are also numerous mineral springs in Slovenia.

The recipes of grandmothers and great-grandmothers and the regions where these culinary delights first appeared. This is the story of Slovenian regions and towns, natural beauty, folk creativity, different fields of everyday life, customs, leisure time, even the spiritual perception of the world in a certain Slovenian region. This is the Slovenian culinary heritage, diverse, a heritage that enriches our present and our future. Cheers to diversity, and may you enjoy a good Slovenian appetite!

Ljubljanica River.
Photo: Dunja Wedam/www.slovenia.info

LJUBLJANA AND THE SURROUNDING AREA

Slovenia's capital city is Ljubljana. There is a lot of love in its name ("ljubljena" is Slovenian for "loved"). During Roman times, there was a Roman settlement in what is now the city centre, and this speaks of a story going back more than two thousand years.

The medieval city centre of Ljubljana lies between the Ljubljanica River and the hill on which stands Ljubljana Castle. The cosmopolitan look of the city is thanks mainly to the architects Jože Plečnik (1872-1957) and Maks Fabiani (1865-1962). The two of them are regarded as Slovenia's leading architects.

The capital city features plenty of museums, galleries, parks, picturesque streets and squares, bridges, an opera house, multiple theatres, a botanical garden and zoo. The city and its central Tivoli Park and surrounding hills offer a lot of scope for recreation. And the magnificent backdrop to the capital city is the Kamnik-Savinja Alps.

The area surrounding Ljubljana also holds a lot of interest. Stretching all the way from the southern margin of Ljubljana to the town of Vrhnika is the Ljubljansko Barje Nature Park, where the oldest wooden wheel and axle in the world have been found. Soon after that, the terrain of the Karst opens up. Heading southeast from Ljubljana, you enter the green basin of Grosuplje. Close by is a karstic cave – Županova jama – near which stands a Gothic church with a preserved camp fortification dating back to the time of Ottoman incursions. Nearby is also the Renaissance castle of Turjak and the town of Rašica, birthplace of Primož Trubar, who was the founder of the Slovenian literary language and literature.

Kamnik, which is just over 20 kilometres from Ljubljana, is one of the most beautiful and oldest medieval towns in Slovenia. It lies at the foot of the Kamnik-Savinja Alps. Close by is the unique Velika planina pasture, with its old preserved dairy herder settlement and cheese- making tradition.

BARLEY MUSH HOTPOT WITH RUNNER BEANS
RIČET Z LAŠKIM FIŽOLOM

Scarlet runner beans were rather popular among our ancestors due to their high nutritional value and complex carbohydrates packed in a thick skin, which enabled easy storing during winter months. A perfect ingredient for seasonal dishes, it was also a staple food during the times of hardship, when households had to deal with food scarcity. It was well known throughout Slovenian regions, although local names for this type of kidney bean vary.

25 dag (9oz) pot barley
50 dag (1lb 2oz) cured smoked meat
1 onion
3 cloves of garlic
1–2 carrots
20 dag (7oz) scarlet runner beans
2 medium sized tomatoes
Olive oil
8 peppercorns, thyme, parsley, salt

Preparation:
1. In a large pot filled with water, add the pot barley, salt and beans that have been soaking overnight.
2. Fry the onions in a pan with olive oil, add and fry the garlic.
3. When the garlic aroma develops, add the sliced carrot and the cured meat, fry for 1 - 2 min.
4. Add the whole mixture to the pot with barley, add the seasoning and other ingredients.
5. Cook for about 1 hour.
6. Keep adding water during cooking to prevent sticking.

FROG SOUP WITH WINE
ŽABJA VINSKA JUHA

Records show that the inhabitants of Ljubljana were enjoying this speciality since the beginning of the 16th century, thanks to proximity of the Barje marshlands. Throughout the history, frog legs were consumed during fasting periods. Even though frogs are now enjoying protection, it is still considered a typical delicacy from Ljubljana.

15 - 20 frog legs
1 tbsp. flour
2 tbsp. butter
2 large potatoes
3 dl white wine
Juice from ½ lemon
Parsley, marjoram, black pepper, salt

Preparation:
1. Gently rub the frog legs with salt and pepper, cover with parsley stalks and leave to marinate for at least 2 hours.
2. Boil the diced potatoes in salted water.
3. Remove the meat from the marinade and finely chop parsley, save the marinade juice for cooking.
4. Melt the butter and quickly fry the flour till golden, add the frog legs and parsley.
5. Fry till golden, add the marinade juice, after a few minutes add the potatoes together with hot water in which they were cooked.
6. Add the seasoning and lemon juice.
7. Cook for about 15 min.

EGG DISH FROM LJUBLJANA
LJUBLJANSKA JAJČNA JED

This is the first case of geographically recognized dish that was mentioned by Magdalena Pleiweis in her 1868 cookbook, which has had numerous improvements and updates for its 28 reprints so far.

5 hard boiled eggs
3 fresh eggs
15 dag (5,5oz) mushrooms
10 dag (3,5oz) white bread
½ cup of milk
Various herbs
2 tsp sour cream
Lemon zest
2 tbsp. breadcrumbs
1 tbsp. lard
Parsley, salt

Preparation:
1. Chop the mushrooms, fry, add the parsley and salt.
2. Halve the boiled eggs, remove and mash yolks.
3. Slice the egg whites into stripes.
4. Mix the fresh and mashed yolks; beat the egg whites into a firm foam, mix.
5. Grease the ceramic baking dishes with butter.
6. Place layer upon layer of the egg yolk mixture, the mushrooms and the egg white stripes, repeat.
7. Bake in the oven at 180'C (350'F) for about 20 min.

BEEF TONGUE WITH FRIED POTATOES
GOVEJI JEZIK S PRAŽENIM KROMPIRJEM

Ever since the 19th century, a sliced beef tongue with horseradish and sometimes with fried potatoes was a treat that accompanied Sunday lunch. Served warm or cold, it could not be omitted from any festive feast, while the art of making a perfect horseradish sauce was also nurtured with great care.

1 beef tongue
Fresh parsley
4 carrots
1 small onion
2 cloves of garlic
Juniper berries
Salt and black pepper
1 tbsp. sugar
2 bay leafs
Horseradish

Potatoes:
 5 potatoes
 3 tbsp. pork lard with cracklings
 2 onions
 Salt, black pepper
 3 tbsp. soup from tongue cooking

Preparation:
1. Place the whole beef tongue into a large pot with salted water.
2. Add the vegetables and seasoning.
3. Cook for about 2 hours (depending on the tongue size).
4. Leave to cool, slice into very thin slices.
5. Peer and grate the horseradish.
6. Boil the whole potatoes.
7. Peel the boiled potatoes and cut into slices.
8. Fry the chopped onions on the lard, add the lard with cracklings.
9. Add the potato slices, seasoning, add the soup from tongue cooking.

LJUBLJANA PANCAKES WITH COTTAGE CHEESE AND TARRAGON
LJUBLJANSKE SKUTNE PALAČINKE S PEHTRANOM

Creation of this dish has probably been aided by abundance of high quality cottage cheese available at the Ljubljana Food Market. Usually prepared during the fresh tarragon season, it was often accompanied with kidney bean soup, or served as a main course on Fridays.

Dough:
2 dl (7oz) milk
2 dl (7oz) water
1 dl (3,5oz) fresh cream
3 eggs
Salt
30 dag (10oz) flour

Coating:
3 eggs
4 dl (14fl oz) fresh cream
Salt

Filling:
30 dag (10oz) cottage cheese
1 dl (3,5fl oz) fresh cream
3 - 5 tbsp. sugar
1 vanilla sugar
1 bunch of fresh tarragon
2 eggs
Salt

Preparation:
1. Prepare the pancake mixture from listed ingredients and make pancakes.
2. Chop the tarragon, mix with the cottage cheese and cream, and add sugar and salt.
3. Add the egg yolks, beat the egg whites and add into the mixture.
4. Fill the pancakes, roll and place into a baking dish.
5. Pour over with the coating and bake for 20 min at 180'C (350' F).

»FIRŠT« GAME MEAT GOULASH
FIRŠTOV DIVJAČINSKI GOLAŽ

This specific game meat goulash brings to our attention the tradition and the social significance of hunting on the outskirts of Kamnik, linked with the Firšt table monument, where dukes had their meals while hunting. It also reminds us of the importance of wild game meat as a culinary speciality, since hunting was reserved only for the ruling classes. Such historic dishes have preserved their historical meaning even after the fall of Austro-Hungarian Empire, when Kamniška Bistrica became the King's court hunting ground, and also later when it became the hunting ground for former Yugoslavia's president Josip Broz – Tito.

0,5 kg (1fl 2oz) game meat
0,5 kg (1fl 2oz) onions
Vegetable oil
15 dag (5,5oz) mushrooms
3 – 5 tbsp. tomato puree
1 tbsp. flour
Mustard, mustard seeds
Parsley, juniper berries, marjoram, bay leaf, nutmeg, ground paprika, rosemary
2 – 3 cloves of garlic
Salt, black pepper

Preparation:
1. Chop and fry the onions.
2. Add the diced meat and fry till softened.
3. Add the chopped mushrooms, tomato puree and seasoning.
4. Sprinkle with flour, add the broth from veal bones.
5. Cook for minimum 1,5 hours.

KAMNIK VEAL TRIPE
RAJŽLC PO KAMNIŠKO

Veal tripe or *rajželjc* used to be regularly on Kamnik townsfolk menus. During the times of Austro – Hungarian Empire, local housewives used to attend prestigious culinary classes in Austrian town of Graz, from where they brought home some improved recipes. *Rajželjc* was often made also with sliced bread in a form of a baked loaf.

0,5 kg (1fl 2oz) veal tripe
2 onions
2 – 3 carrots
2 tbsp. oil
2 – 4 cloves garlic
Tomato puree
Parsley, rosemary, bay leaf, marjoram
Salt, black pepper
1 tsp butter

Veal broth:
Veal bones
Oil
Carrots
Celery root
2 onions

Preparation:
1.   Fry the veal bones on oil, add other ingredients and cook for at least 40 min.
2.   In another pot, fry the onions, add the grated carrots, sauté for 10 min.
3.   Add the chopped veal tripe and other ingredients.
4.   Add the veal broth and cook for additional 30 min or more.
5.   Can be served with cooked fruit.

TUHINJ BREAD STUFFING
T'HINSKA FILA

Tuhinjska fila bread stuffing is linked with one of the most important religious holidays; therefore, it is still prepared mostly during Easter. There are different versions of this dish, with the most famous being the one which includes baking in dough and pork fat netting. It has been listed among Kamink culinary strategy dishes which enhance local festive menu and help with the transfer of knowledge.

45 dag (1lb) boiled ham
10 dag (3,5oz) buns
45 dag (1lb) white bread
1 dl (3,5fl oz) fresh cream
6 eggs
Garlic, cumin, chives, parsley, salt, black pepper
Pork fat netting

Preparation:
1. Boil the buns and the ham.
2. Chop the bread and cooled ham.
3. Pour over the egg yolks, cream and water from ham cooking, season to taste.
4. Beat the egg whites, add to the mixture right before placing into a baking dish.
5. Unfold the pork fat netting, fill with the mixture and fold.
6. Bake in the oven at 160'C (325'F) for 30 min.
7. Leave to cool for about 1 hour, then cut into slices.
8. Can be served with horseradish.

Otočec Castle,
Photo: Terme Krka Archives

DOLENJSKA, BELA KRAJINA AND KOČEVSKO

Dolenjska is a region in southeast Slovenia. The central part of Dolenjska is a hilly landscape along the River Krka and its tributaries, where many animal and plant species have found refuge. The attractiveness of this landscape lies also in the heritage of former mills and sawmills, the preserved wooden bridges and the settlements along the banks. The valley of the River Krka also boasts many ancient castles, of which the castle at Otočec stands out.

The economic and cultural centre of Dolenjska is Novo mesto, where the Dolenjska Museum offers a view of many architectural features of interest. The most distinctive finds are situlas, which have lent Novo mesto the name Town of Situlas.

At the foot of the Gorjanci range lies Kostanjevica na Krki, the smallest town and only one on an island, also referred to as the Dolenjska Venice. Close by you can tour the Kostanjevica or Studena cave. The island is adorned with the thickest willow in Slovenia, and the Gorjanci mountains make a lovely excursion.

Kočevsko is the part of Dolenjska around the towns of Ribnica and Kočevje, and is home to traditional wooden ware, known locally under the name of suha roba, as well as pottery. The Kočevje area is covered by vast forests, the largest primeval woodland in Europe and a protected area since 1888, where many wild animals live, including the brown bear, wolf and lynx.

Bela krajina is the land of white birches and Zeleni Jurij (the Green Man figure), and it is also famous for its painted Easter eggs and numerous other old customs. The green landscape layered with vineyards and deciduous forests conceals many caves and sinkholes, and it is dotted with churches, stone cottages and hay drying racks.

DUMPLINGS FROM DOLENJSKA REGION
ŽLINKROFI

Žlinkrofi or dumplings arrived to this area during the 18th and 19th century migrations of miners from Eastern Europe. Pouches of dough are classified according to a specific regional filling. Today, the most famous are the Idrija dumplings (*Idrijski žlikrofi*) which have been certified as "Traditional Speciality Guaranteed" by the European Commission.

Dough:
50 (1lb 2oz) dag white flour
2 eggs
2 tbsp. cream
1 tbsp. oil
1 pinch of salt
Lukewarm water, as needed

Filling:
0,75 l (1,25 pints) milk
15 dag (5,5oz) millet, cooked
2 dl (0,5pints) sour cream
50 dag (1lb 2oz) boiled cured meat
3 eggs
Chives, salt

Preparation:
1. Make a pliable dough and leave to rest for 30 minutes.
2. Chop the meat and add other ingredients
3. Thinly roll out the dough and cut into squares 5x5 cm.
4. Place the filling on one half of each square, fold it and stick the edges together.
5. Make an indentation on top to achieve a typical shape.
6. Boil in salted water for approx. 10 minutes.
7. Drain, pour over the hot cream and sprinkle with the chives.

HOLIDAY BREAD
PLETENICE

Bread braid was made as a richer, gently sweet variety of bread for special festive occasions. The braid had to be made with four strains weaving. It was a typical gift for one's name day or for a bride, who received it along with other goodies in a basket as a token for good fortune as well as a food ration for her first week of marriage and life in a new home.

50 dag (1lb 2oz) flour
3 tbsp. oil
1 tbsp. sugar
Rum
1 egg
1 egg yolk for crust
1 vanilla sugar
3 tbsp. warm milk
3 tbsp. dl lukewarm cream
1 teaspoon cream of tartar
2 dag (7oz) yeast
Salt

Preparation:
1.   In a bowl, mix the flour, cream of tartar and yeast, salt, warm milk, oil and cream.
2.   Whisk the egg, add sugar, vanilla sugar and rum.
3.   Mix together, make a fluffy dough and let rise for 30 – 40 minutes.
4.   Cut the dough into several pieces and roll them into long ropes
5.   Use 4 for each braid, coat each braid with the egg yolk
6.   Bake for 30 minutes at 180' C (350' F).

ROLLED STRUKLI FROM KOSTEL
KOSTELSKI ŠTRUKLJI

Štruklji or Strukli used to be a daily staple in Dolenjska region, from where this dish had spread to other regions with varieties in filling and dough quality affected by family status and available ingredients. Although ingredients were rather modest, this dish was a welcomed improvement of their limited menu varieties.

50 dag (1lb 2oz) flour
5-6 tbsp. pork lard
Cumin, whole
Salt
Water

Preparation:
1. Make a pliable dough from the flour, water, salt and 1 tbsp. lard.
2. Leave to rest for at least 30 min, roll the dough 2 - 3 mm thick, spread most of the leftover lard on top.
3. Roll into thinner layer, spread some more lard and sprinkle with cumin.
4. Fold into a snail-shape and boil in salted water for 20 min.

BELA KRAJINA ROLLED CAKE
BELOKRANJSKA POVITICA

The name *povitica*, coming from the verb for 'wrap', tells us this is a dish that is wrapped or rolled up, like many in Slovenia. But here we are dealing with a protected food that was supposedly brought to our lands by Uskok (people who fled from he Balkans due to Otoman Empire invasions), and is reminiscent of *burek* from the lands of Slovenia's southern neighbours. Since researching our food heritage yields diverse details and variations from village to village, alongside its customary fillings, povitica can be found with additions such as fat, pork rinds or buckwheat mash.

Dough:
  200 g flour
  1 dl water
  1 egg
  1 tbsp oil
  A pinch of salt

Filling:
  200 g fat-free cottage cheese
  1 tbsp sugar
  60 g softened butter
  1 egg
  2 tbsp crème brulee
  A pinch of salt

Preparation:
1. In a large bowl mix in the ingredients for the dough, mix well and form a little loaf.
2. Baste the loaf with oil, place in a small pan and cover.
3. Let the dough sit for at least half an hour.
4. Spread a large cloth on the counter top and sprinkle evenly with flour.
5. Place the loaf on the cloth and roll it out into a rectangle.
6. Then stretch the dough out by hand until you can almost see through it (less than 5 mm thick).
7. Cut off the edges of the dough.
8. In a separate dish mix the ingredients for the filling and spread them evenly over the stretched dough.
9. Using the cloth, roll the dough into a 'snail', then shape into a rotolo.
10. Grease a round baking tin and place the rotolo on it, then baste with butter.
11. Heat the oven to 180 °C, and bake the povitica at this temperature for 40 minutes.
12. Serve hot.

BELA KRAJINA FLAT CAKE
BELOKRANJSKA POGAČA

Supposedly this dish is the result of intercultural influences and the arrival of various peoples or cultures in the area of Slovenia. Belokranjska pogača is one of the officially protected dishes with a traditional reputation. Since March 2010 it has also been protected in the European Union.

750 g soft flour
3 dl water
A little oil
40 g yeast
3 pinches of salt
Coarse salt for garnish
Caraway seeds
Egg for coatings

Preparation:
1. Mix up dough with the flour, water, oil, yeast and salt.
2. Cover and leave to rise for 30 minutes.
3. Then roll it into a 2 cm thick sheet and spread with beaten egg.
4. Using a knife, lightly carve the distinctive web on the surface.
5. Sprinkle the dough with coarse salt and caraway seeds.
6. Bake in a preheated oven for 30 minutes at 180 °C.

Sevnica.
Photo: Iztok Medja/www.slovenia.info

POSAVJE AND ZASAVJE

The centre of the Posavje region is the town of Brežice. Posavje is a region along the Sava River centred around Brežice, while more recently Sevnica has become an increasingly prominent local town. Slovenia can boast many castles, and one of these gems is Sevnica Castle, regarded as one of the most important castles in Slovenia. A proper castle vineyard has been planted on the castle slopes.

Posavje is famous for its thermal springs that were discovered more than 200 years ago; their powers were soon recognised as therapeutic. Today there are numerous spas here.
A wander around the rolling hills of Brežice municipality can also be a wonderful gastronomic experience, since the Podgorjanska and Bizeljsko–Sremiška wine roads wind their way through the area. Another unforgettable experience is a guided tour to the cradle of Cviček wine – Gadova peč.

Running through the town of Bistrica by the Sotla River is the Bistrica River, which boasts one of the most beautiful gorges in Slovenia. Owing to the diversity of natural features and preserved plant and animal habitats, and given its extraordinary cultural heritage, the entire municipality of Bistrica ob Sotli falls within the Kozjansko Regional Park.

Zasavje is an area in the heart of the Posavje hills on the extreme south-eastern margin of the Savinja Alps, and is at the same time in the heart of Slovenia. The towns of Hrastnik, Trbovlje and Zagorje ob Savi bear the distinct stamp of mining towns. Their surrounding areas have preserved a lot of rural traditions and natural and cultural features. Close to Litija is the town of Vače, famous for its situla, a priceless find from the Iron Age. In nearby Spodnja Slivna is the Geoss, the geometric centre of Slovenia. There is a nice excursion from Litija to the Renaissance castle of Bogenšperk, which is one of the best-preserved castles in Slovenia.

RABBIT STEW WITH PASTA POCKETS
ZAJČJI AJMOHT S TESTENIMI ŽEPKI

Due to its geographical attributes, the mining-based economy and widespread poverty, which all worked against raising livestock, the desire for meat was satisfied mostly by hunting. Due to the high altitudes, the most common catch was rabbits, hence the local specialities which we admire today were common people's staple food back in the old days. Rabbit's liver was used for special sausages which are still to be found only in the Zasavje area.

Soup:
 1 kg (2.25lb) rabbit thighs, deboned
 850 g (30z) bacon
 2 red and 2 yellow carrots
 1 kohlrabi, celery root, 2 parsley roots, ½ onion
 5 cloves of garlic
 3 tbsp oil
 1 dl (3.5fl oz) white wine
 1 dl (3.5fl oz) sour cream
 4 tbsp flour
 Fresh chives and parsley, marjoram
 Bay leaf, summer savory, nutmeg
 Salt, black pepper

Dough for pockets:
 500 g (1lb 2oz) flour
 5 eggs
 Salt

Filling:
 100 g (3.5oz) rabbit liver
 Chunk of onion
 3 tbsp white wine
 1 tbsp fresh cream
 Marjoram, black pepper, thyme, parsley

Preparation:
1. Fry the chopped onion in hot oil, add chopped rabbit meat, bacon, vegetables and garlic.
2. Add the water and wine, add the seasoning and cook until the meat is tender.
3. Heat the oil in a pan, add the flour and stir, mix into the soup when done.
4. Add the sour cream upon serving.

Dough pockets:
1. Chop the onion and rabbit liver, fry. Add the seasoning, garlic, wine and fresh cream.
2. Mince the liver mixture.
3. Roll the pasta dough 2 mm thick and cut into circles. Fill the circles with the minced liver mixture, fold and stick the edges, cook in salty boiling water.
4. Add the cooked pockets to the stew.

PASTA WITH POTATOES
GRENEDIRMARŠ

Such an interesting name originates from German, from the era of the Austro-Hungarian Empire when this dish was served to soldiers – even during WW1. Later, this dish was popular among workmen from countries north of Slovenia who migrated to the Zasavje area to work in the mines or glass factory.

500 g (1lb 2oz) potatoes
300 g (10oz) wide flat pasta
1 onion
Piece of bacon
Lard with cracklings
Salt, pepper, marjoram, thyme

Preparation:
1. Boil the whole potatoes.
2. Chop the onion and fry in the lard, add the sliced boiled potatoes.
3. Fry till golden brown and mix with the boiled pasta.
4. Add the cracklings, herbs and spices.

BREAD - EGG OMELETTE OR MINER'S SUN
KRUHOV FUNŠTERC ALI KNAPOVSKO SONCE

This egg dish from Zasavje is recognized as a part of the local gastronomy heritage strategy. It is also referred to under the name Miner's Sun, both because of its round appearance and its purpose. It has been considered a treat and a superb nourishment fit for miners to take with them to work. Oftentimes rats would steal food out of miner's pockets, so they made jokes that an elf named *Perkmandeljc* was playing tricks on them. Although keeping hens was widespread, eggs were not considered a staple food but rather a treat. *Funšterc* served with salad makes a hearty lunch or dinner even today, despite some changes in our dietary habits. The following version of the recipe is an enriched one.

5 eggs
200 g (7oz) rabbit liver
1 onion
2 tbsp lard with cracklings
300 g (10oz) bread
2 dl (7fl oz) milk
Salt, black pepper, nutmeg

Preparation:
1. Dice the onion and fry in the lard, add the chopped liver.
2. Add the seasoning, cook and leave to cool.
3. Break the bread white into chunks, in a bowl mix with the milk and egg yolks.
4. Beat the egg whites until firm.
5. Mix the bread and liver, add the egg whites.
6. Make patties and fry them in the lard with cracklings, on both sides.
7. Serve with a salad.

FRIED MILK MUSH
ZAROŠTAN MLEČNI MOČNIK

This simple meal became a true folk-dish which found its place in almost every home in Slovenia. Yet, if we take a close look, each mush has a specific regional taste and an individual cook's touch. Unrecognizable to most, some differences in preparation and ingredients are crucial to connoisseurs.

15 dag (5,5oz) wheat flour
1 egg
125 g (4,5oz) butter
1 apple
Vanilla sugar
Salt
2 l (3,5pints) milk
Optional – apple puree

Preparation:
1. Whisk the egg, mix with the flour and make a firm dough.
2. Mix with fork until the dough crumbles into large chunks then crush into even smaller crumbs with your fingers.
3. Heat the butter in a pan, fry most of the dough crumbs till golden brown.
4. Pour the cold milk over the crumbs, add salt, place on a stove.
5. Once the milk reaches the boiling point, add the rest of the dough crumbs and cook on low heat for 15 minutes.
6. Peel and grate the apple, mix with the cooked mush.

BOŠTANJ STUFFED APPLE
POLNJENA BOŠTANJSKA VOŠČENKA

Before the WW2, the Boštanj area had popular and very active farmers associations with branches across their current state borders. One of the most prominent was the association of fruit farmers, which managed to produce a new unique sort of apple named Boštanj Yellow Waxy apple. This fruit had become a staple of local cuisine and a symbol of their identity so much, that it adorns the coat of arms of Boštanj.

4 apples

Filling:
  30 dag (10oz) ground walnuts
  2 tbsp. raisins
  1 tbsp. sugar
  1 egg
  Tbsp. rum
  Lemon juice

Preparation:
1.   Core the apples, keep them in one piece, with the bottoms intact.
2.   Remove some more of the apple centre to make enough room for 1 tbsp. of filling.
3.   Mix the walnuts with other ingredients for filling and stuff the apples.
4.   Bake in the oven at 250'C (450'F) for 30 min.
5.   Sprinkle with honey or powdered sugar.

Kozjansko Regional Park.
Photo: Jošt Gantar/www.slovenia.info

KOZJANSKO AND BIZELJSKO

The central part of eastern Slovenia is a hilly landscape. It covers the eastern section of the Posavje hills along the Bistrica River. In the east it borders the Sotla River, while its western margin is the tributaries of the Sava and Savinja rivers. The region is known for Kozjansko Regional Park, the majority of which is included in the Natura 2000 area. As many as 120 different bird species live here. The natural heritage also includes dry grassland and tall-trunk orchards, the Planina castle park, a bird refuge on Lake Slivnica, the cave of Gruška jama and the picturesque Ajdovska žena rock face. In addition to the numerous castles and old mills, the special sites of interest in this area include the Olimje Monastery. The park is also home to the biggest oak tree in Slovenia, which is 32 m high and has a circumference of 8 m.

Bizeljsko is a gentle landscape of rolling hills in the hinterland of Brežice in southeast Slovenia, and is famous for wine-growing. Related to this is one of the main features of Bizeljsko – the *repnice*. These are more than 200 year-old sand caves of silicate sand that are among the native, natural, historical, ethnological and cultural heritage of this area. At one time they were used for winter stores, and people also stored wine in them. Bizeljsko Castle is another site of special interest.

One of the most beloved popularised Slovenian poems is "En hribček bom kupil" (I will buy a little hill). The wonderful poem, dedicated to "sweet wine", was written by the nationally conscious Slovenian bishop, writer and poet Anton Martin Slomšek. Few people know that the poem originated in Bizeljsko.

CARROT SOUP
KOREJEVEC

Originally made with yellow and white carrots, nowadays it's made also with the red variety. A typical late autumn and winter dish, especially if a supply of carrots was abundant.

45 dag (1lb) carrots
30 dag (10oz) kidney beans
2 shallots
2 tablespoons (tbsp.) pork lard with cracklings
4 cloves of garlic
2 tbsp. of cider vinegar
Bay leaf, marjoram, sweet paprika
Salt, black pepper

Preparation:
1. Soak the kidney beans overnight and cook in salted water till half-cooked.
2. Add the thinly sliced carrots, chopped garlic, shallots and spices.
3. Continue cooking for about 30 min, till cooked and thickened.
4. Add the lard with cracklings, bring to boil.
5. Upon serving, add some vinegar.

BIZELJSKO BUCKWHEAT CAKE
BIZELJSKI AJDOV KOLAČ

Buckwheat cake is one of the symbols of Bizeljsko, an authentic culinary feature of this region. Local homemakers used to prepare it for Easter and All Saints Day, as well as for Christmas dinner where it was an obligatory dessert. Every year in Bizeljsko region, there is an exhibition with culinary competition, which motivates younger cooks, and helps preserve local gastronomic culture.

Dough:
50 dag (1lb 2oz) buckwheat flour
17,5 dag (6oz) hard wheat flour
2 dl (7fl oz) sour cream
1,5 l (2,25 pints) water

Filling:
1,8 kg (4lb) cottage cheese
3 eggs
Salt
15 dag (5,5oz) butter
Sour cream for crust

Preparation:
1. Add salt to the buckwheat flour, pour in the hot water, leave to cool, add the hard flour and sour cream.
2. Make the dough then divide into two or three parts.
3. Make the filling from listed ingredients.
4. Roll out the dough into thin sheets, cover with the filling and small chunks of butter.
5. Roll the dough and place it into a greased baking pan.
6. Bake for 20 min at 200'C (400'F), continue for 20 min more at 160'C (325'F).
7. Coat the cake with the sour cream and bake utill finished.
8. Leave to cool for easier cutting.

CORN CAKE
PRGA - PRŠJAČA

Corn cake is the most popular type of cake in Posavje region. Made of raised corn dough, it perfectly accompanies dandelion salad or chicory coffee, improves one's Sunday breakfast and feeds the vineyard or farm workers. Today it is predominantly found on the menus of farms, which cater to tourists.

Dough:
  50 dag (1lb 2oz) corn flour
  3 dl (10fl oz) milk
  1 dl (3,5fl oz) cream (plain or sour)
  1 egg
  5 dag (1,75oz) yeast
  Teaspoon (tbsp.) of salt

Filling:
  50 dag (1lb 2oz) cottage cheese
  2 tbsp. sour cream
  2 eggs
  Grease for baking pan

Preparation:
1. Mix the milk and cream, bring to boil and pour into a bowl with the flour.
2. Add salt, mix thoroughly and leave to cool.
3. Once cooled, add the egg and crushed yeast.
4. Mix and add enough milk (or cream) to achieve smooth consistency.
5. Add the filling for better taste.
6. Pour into a greased baking pan and bake for 30 minutes at 180' C (350'F).

BIZELJSKO FLAT CAKE TART
BIZELJSKA MLINČEVKA

Layered cake "Mlinčevka" was a dessert of choice for festive occasions, made by housewives for weddings, jubilees, holidays or harvest related events. Made with cottage cheese filling between layers of *mlinci* pasta sheets, it is a special local culinary feature.

Leavened dough:
  30 dag (10oz) white flour
  1 dl (3,5fl oz) milk
  2 dag 0,75oz) yeast
  2 tbsp. sugar
  2 egg yolks
  1 tbsp. dag butter
  Lemon zest

Baked pasta *mlinci*:
  20 dag (7oz) white flour
  1 egg
  4 tbsp. water
  Salt
  Hot milk

Filling:
  50 dag (1lb 2oz) cottage cheese
  15 dag (5,5oz) sugar
  1 vanilla sugar
  Lemon zest
  2 eggs
  20 dag (7oz) ground walnuts
  2 dl (7fl oz) sour cream
  2 tbsp. raisins
  Cinnamon

Preparation:
1. Make the leavened dough, spread it to cover the inside of a deep baking pan.
2. Make the pasta dough, spread into thin slices the size of a baking pan and bake in the oven till dry and crisp.
3. When the baked pasta sheets are cool, pour the hot milk over them.
4. Combine the filling ingredients.
5. Add a thin layer of the filling into a baking pan covered with dough, cover with a layer of drained baked pasta - repeat till supply lasts.
6. Leave to rise for 20 min, pour over with the cream and bake for 45 min at 180'C (350'F).

The oldest grapevine in the world.
Photo: Domen Grögl/STA

PODRAVJE

This region lies along the Drava River and its tributaries. The valley along the river is rich in forests and surface waters that flow into the Drava. In these areas the hydroenergy power of the river was always important. Agriculture became continually more focused on commercial forestry. Glassmaking, mining, charcoal making and ironworking were also important. Podravje is famous too for its vineyards, and its natural features are favourable for grapevine cultivation.

Maribor is the second largest city in Slovenia and the capital of the Štajerska region. The city lies between wine-producing hills and the forested slopes of the Pohorje. The symbiosis of the city and the grapevine is affirmed by the 400-year old vine of the local žametovka variety, which grows in the Lent Quarter of the city on the left bank of the River Drava. It is the oldest grapevine in the world.

Close to Maribor is the Pohorje, a low mountain chain that is densely forested. At one time here there were herders, glassmakers and ironworks, while today it hosts Slovenia's biggest ski run, Mariborsko Pohorje, with more than 40 km of pistes. The ski centre also boasts the longest illuminated piste in Europe. It is known around the world for the Zlata lisica (Golden Fox) women's skiing world cup.

One of the bigger centres of the Podravje region is Ptuj, Slovenia's oldest town. The most prominent features of the town are its medieval castle and the oldest wine cellar in Slovenia. A distinctive feature of the town and the entire Ptuj area is the kurent, an original Shrovetide Carnival character supposed to chase winter away.

Not far from Ptuj is one of the most outstanding buildings of its time, the Žiče Charterhouse, which evolved into a unique cultural and historical monument. By the monastery entrance stands Gastuž, Slovenia's oldest inn (founded in 1467), which to this day keeps medieval recipes.

BEAN GOULASH
FIŽOLOV GOLAŽ

Throughout history, kidney beans were the main substitute for meat and were easy to combine with a variety of other ingredients; they are therefore found in a variety of dishes in all Slovenian regions. Thanks to Catherine De Medici, a member of the nobility who used to enjoy goulash, the dish was removed from their menus due to the unpleasant consequences of eating beans. After that, the dish became a staple food in farmer and working class households.

1 kg (2.25lb) beans
4 onions
2 cloves of garlic
2 carrots
Piece of celery root
200 g (7oz) fresh pork
300 g (10oz) cured smoked pork
Tomato puree
2 tbsp lard
Ground paprika, bay leaf, thyme
Salt, black pepper

Preparation:
1. Soak the beans overnight and boil in salted water.
2. Chop the vegetables and the meat.
3. Fry the onions and garlic in the lard, add the meat and vegetables and season.
4. Sauté for 15 min, add the beans with some water from cooking.
5. Add the tomato puree and cook until the meat is tender.

TURNIP FLATCAKE
REPJAČA

This dish is one of several authentic dishes of the northeast of Slovenia. Just like most other local dishes, it was named after the stuffing, which is determined by either seasonal ingredient, local custom or availability. This dish was on the menu predominantly during the All Saints Day holiday. The closest cousin of this dish is *tikvača*, filled with pumpkin or other type of squash.

Dough:
300 g (10oz) buckwheat flour
150 g (5.5oz) hard wheat flour
2 dl (7fl oz) boiling water
Salt
3 tbsp oil

Filling:
450 g (1lb) fresh grated turnip
1 l (1.75 pint) milk for soaking
300 g (10oz) cottage cheese
2.4 dl (8fl oz) sour cream
2 tbsp sugar
Pinch of cinnamon and cloves

Coating:
1 egg
4 – 5 tbsp sour cream

Preparation:
1. Pour the salted boiling water over the buckwheat flour and leave for half an hour.
2. Add other ingredients and make a pliable smooth dough.
3. Leave for at least half an hour.
4. Roll the dough 3 mm thick and cut in two
5. One day earlier, peel and grate the turnip, cook for about half an hour in salted water with cinnamon and cloves.
6. Strain the cold turnip and soak overnight in milk.
7. Strain the turnip and blend with the other filling ingredients.
8. Spread the filling over half of the dough placed in a greased baking pan.
9. Cover with the other half of the dough and spread over the sour cream mixed with the egg.
10. Bake in the oven at 180° C (350° F) for about 35 min.

CORN CAKE
KORUZJAČA

This is a sophisticated version of all sorts of flat cakes and cornbread filled with curd and apples – local staple ingredients. This specific recipe was obtained through oral lore, and enhanced with the rich legacy of creatively combining basic ingredients into a practical – or in this case trendy – dish.

250 g (9oz) corn grits
6 apples
4 dl (14fl oz) sour cream
300 g (10oz) cottage cheese
1 egg
6 tbsp sugar
Butter
Cinnamon, salt

Preparation:
1. Cook the grits in salted boiling water for 10 min, then pour into greased moulds.
2. Mix the cottage cheese with sugar and spread a thick layer on top of the grits.
3. Grate the apple, mix with the cinnamon and spread on top of the cottage cheese.
4. Beat the egg with cream and some sugar according to taste, and pour on top.
5. Bake in the oven at 150° C (300° F) for about 10 min, until the cream on top becomes brownish.

COOKED STRUDEL IN SOUP
ŠTRUKLJI V JUHI

Preparation of *Štruklji* with cottage cheese has spread throughout Slovenia, with some slight variations in preparation technique. In this case we are dealing with the legacy of the Drava valley inhabitants and their aim of serving a dish which delivers an entire lunch – the soup and the main course.

Dough:
  500 g (1fl 2oz) white flour
  1 egg
  4 dl (14fl oz) warm water
  Salt

Coating:
  4 eggs
  2 tbsp pork
  Cracklings
  Water

Filling:
  4 eggs
  500 g (1fl 2oz) full-fat cottage cheese
  4 full tablespoons of breadcrumbs
  2 tbsp butter

Preparation:
1. Knead the dough, spread the oil over and leave for 2 hours.
2. Fry the breadcrumbs in the butter and mix with other ingredients for the filling.
3. Roll the dough as thin as possible, cover with the filling and roll.
4. Cut the roll into 4 – 5 cm long pieces.
5. Boil the parsley in salted water, add the Štruklji rolls and cook together for 15 min.
6. Heat the cracklings in a pan, fry the scrambled egg and add to the soup.
7. Sprinkle with some fresh parsley, according to taste.

SCRAP CAKE
POSTRŽAČA

A very typical traditional snack enjoyed by our ancestors was *postržača*, which had countless varieties of the base dough and the spread throughout the Slovenian regions. The name reveals that it was made from leftover bread dough and spiced up with any leftovers that could be scraped (*postrgan*) from the pantry in order to make a tasty main course or a snack to be served with a glass of wine.

Dough:
300 g (10oz) buckwheat flour
150 g (5.5oz) hard wheat flour
3.5 dl (12fl oz) warm water
1 block of yeast
Salt

Filling:
3 tbsp minced lard
3 tbsp cracklings
1 onion
2 stems of parsley
1 lemon

Preparation:
1. Dissolve the yeast in 1 dl of warm water and leave for a few minutes to rise.
2. In a large bowl, mix the flour, add the yeast and salt.
3. Knead the dough until it stops sticking to the bowl and later stops sticking to the kneading board.
4. Place the dough back in the bowl, cover with kitchen towel and leave to rise for at least half an hour.
5. In a pan, melt the minced lard and fry the cracklings.
6. Finally add the onion and lemon juice.
7. Roll the dough 2 mm thick, place in a baking pan and leave to rise for 15 min.
8. Bake at 190° C (375° F) for 15 min.
9. While the cake is still warm, spread the filling and roll.
10. Leave to partially cool, then cut into wide pieces.

LEAVENED APPLE STRUDEL
KVAŠENI JABOLČNI ŠTRUDELJ

In a land where bread is a staple food, pieces of leavened dough were taken away during bread making, and turned into all sorts of flatbreads, rolls, cakes, doughnuts etc. Leavened strudel or roll, which originates from neighbouring Austria, has been transformed into a more filling dish.

Dough:
 0.5 kg (1fl 2oz) flour
 Sourdough starter: 1 tbsp fresh yeast, 3 tbsp warm milk, 1 tsp sugar
 Milk as needed
 Some butter or lard
 Salt

Filling:
 1 kg (2.25lb) apples
 300 g (10oz) ground walnuts
 Sugar

Preparation:
1.   Make the sourdough starter, mix with the flour and make the dough.
2.   Leave the dough for at least 40 min.
3.   Peel and grate the apples, mix with the sugar.
4.   Roll the dough 3mm thick, sprinkle with the apples and walnuts then roll.
5.   Leave to rise for 20 min.
6.   Bake in the oven at 180° C (350° F) for about 40 min.

Church in Bogojina, designed by the architect Jože Plečnik.
Photo: Jošt Gantar/www.slovenia.info

PREKMURJE AND PRLEKIJA

For centuries, Prekmurje was known for its typical straw-thatched low Pannonian houses. The floating mills on the Mura River are also associated with this region. It is also a land of storks, which are the symbol of Prekmurje.

It lies on the eastern side of the Mura River, in the far northeast of the country. Goričko, where there is also a nature park, lies on the tri-border area between Slovenia, Hungary and Austria. It descends into the lowland plains (Ravensko, Dolinsko) of southern Prekmurje, and over the Mura it shifts into the hill country of Slovenske Gorice. Prekmurje is also special for its distinctive Slovenian dialect, which has always been under great pressure from neighbouring countries.

There are numerous natural spas with thermal water here. Healing waters spring to the surface in Radenci (Radenska), Banovci, Moravci, Lendava and elsewhere. This region has no lack of a good drop of wine, which together with the Prekmurska gibanica cake, other treats and the friendliness of the people draw in visitors from near and far.

Neighbouring Prlekija lies in north-eastern Slovenia between the hills of Slovenske Gorice and the Mura River. It is centred around Ljutomer. This area is also well-known for its wine-making, and is home to some major wine cellars in Ljutomer, Ormož and Kapela.

The ethnological features of this area include wind rattles, mills and rope ferries. The klopotec wind rattle is a little wooden windmill placed on a high pole in vineyards to scare away birds. Since for the most part Prlekija has always been a farming area, a lot of mills can be found here. One of the most famous is the Babič Mill, which has stood on the Mura River since 1890.

This is also a home to traditional cottage crafts: barrel-making, blacksmithing, pottery and stove-making, mead, carving and wickerwork.

PICKLED TURNIP WITH MILLET MUSH
BUJTA REPA

This dish is one of the most famous typical gastronomical peculiarities of the region, and has been preserved until present times. Turnip is one of the most common ingredients used in north-eastern Slovenia, and was usually pickled for winter. Typical during pig slaughtering and meat processing, it required a piece of meat, preferably from the pig's head. The quality of the dish used to be measured by the thickness of grease on top.

1 kg (2.25lb) pickled turnip
1 kg (2.25lb) pork meat
250 g (9oz) millet
1 tbsp flour
1 large onion
2 cloves garlic
Lard
Peppercorns, bay leaves, ground paprika, salt

Preparation:
1.   Dice the meat into small cubes, boil in salted water together with the turnip.
2.   Fry the onions and garlic in lard, add flour, then some water.
3.   After 40 min. add the onions, garlic, millet and paprika.
4.   Cook until the millet grains break.

PREKMURJE GOULASH
BOGRAČ

A famous local traditional version of goulash. The rule that must be respected is that there should be at least three types of meat, and the onions should be fried in pork lard. It is still a staple food for birthdays and other parties in the Prekmurje region. Competitions in preparing this delicious meal are very popular in this region.

500 g (1lb 2oz) beef, deboned
500 g (1lb 2oz) pork
250 g (9oz) game meat
6 medium sized onions
3 cloves garlic
100 g (3.5oz) pork lard
2 red peppers
1 tomato
1 kg (2.25oz) potatoes, peeled
1–2 dl wine
Bay leaf, pinch of thyme, 1 or more chilli
Black pepper, salt, ground paprika, cumin, pimento, marjoram, juniper berries, rosemary

Preparation:
1. Fry the chopped onions in lard till golden, add the beef cut into chunks.
2. Add the chopped red peppers, tomato and paprika.
3. Sauté for 15 min, then add enough water to cover all ingredients and add seasoning.
4. Add the chunks of game meat and grate the two raw potatoes into the pot for thickening.
5. Bring to boil then cook on low heat for 15 min.
6. Add the chunks of pork and cook for 15 min.
7. Add the diced remaining potatoes and wine, cook until the stew thickens and the potatoes are cooked.
8. For spicier taste, add some chilli.

PUMPKIN GOULASH
BUČNI GOLAŽ

The Središče ob Dravi area has been producing pumpkins for a very long time, which contributed to the building of the oil processing factory that makes a high quality pumpkin seed oil. Despite its remoteness, it was exactly through the promotion of pumpkin by-products that this factory contributed to the recognizable public image of the area. For the last 12 years, a pumpkin themed festival has been held in Središče ob Dravi, with a cooking competition in making pumpkin goulash, which has become a tradition and a hallmark of the region.

1 musk or Hokkaido pumpkin
300 g (10oz) pork leg steak
1 large onion
2 yellow carrots and 1 red
2 potatoes
1 green and 1 yellow bell pepper
4 tbsp tomato puree
2 cloves garlic
1 tsp pork lard
Seasonal herbs, salt, black pepper

Preparation:
1. Fry the diced onion in pork lard till transparent, then add the pork meat cut into chunks.
2. Sauté slowly, then add the diced carrots, potatoes, peppers, crushed garlic and tomato puree.
3. Add water and seasonings and cook for about half an hour.
4. Add the diced pumpkin and cook for about 15 min.

BRAWN
ŽOLCA

Pork brawn originates from the Austro-Hungarian Empire. It is a typical speciality of north-eastern Slovenia that is still regularly served with onions, pumpkin seed oil and hard-boiled eggs as a part of almost every festive menu. The essence of pork brawn is pork tallow obtained through slow cooking at low temperatures. Usually, the meat was previously smoked in order to enable better preservation for a longer shelf life.

1 kg (2.25lb) pork skin
4 chopped pork trotters
2 heads of garlic
Bay leaf, ground paprika, salt, black pepper

Preparation:
1. In a large pot, place the pork skin and trotters in cold water, add salt.
2. Simmer slowly and skim off foam as it emerges.
3. Season with the chopped garlic and other seasonings.
4. Cook for 3 – 4 hours or until the meat falls off skin and bones, then remove the bones.
5. Leave the brawn for about 2 hours, then pour into moulds where the gelatinous brawn will harden.
6. Cut and serve sprinkled with some pumpkin seed oil and fresh vegetables.

BUCKWHEAT FLAT CAKE
AJDOV KRAPEC

This specific buckwheat cake must be baked in a round shape even today, in order to respect the tradition. Usually made from bread dough leftovers, it is a typical creation of frugal housewives. The fillings were determined by what was to be found in the pantry. A member of the flat cake family, this recipe is a culinary speciality of the lower flatland areas of the Pomurje region.

Dough:
500 g (1lb 2oz) flour (mix ½ wheat and ½ buckwheat)
Sourdough starter: 45 g (1.5oz) fresh yeast, 3tbsp milk, 1 tbsp sugar.
2.4 dl (8fl oz) lukewarm water
1.5 dl (5fl oz) oil

Topping:
2 dl (7fl oz) sour cream
3–4 tbsp minced lard

Preparation:
1. Place the flour in a large bowl and stir.
2. Mix the sourdough starter and leave to rise.
3. Add the sourdough starter to flour, add lukewarm water.
4. Make the dough and leave to rise for at least half an hour.
5. Roll the dough 5 mm thick and place in a round baking pan.
6. In a skillet, melt the minced lard, add the sour cream and pour over the dough.
7. Bake in a pre-heated oven at 200° C (400° F) for 20 min.
8. Before serving, slice into typical triangles.

Savinja River.
Photo: Matjaž Jambrško/www.slovenia.info

UPPER AND LOWER SAVINJA VALLEY, ŠALEK VALLEY

The Upper Savinja Valley is a typical Alpine landscape, and without doubt one of the most beautiful in Europe. In the headwaters of the Savinja River in Solčavsko the Kamnik-Savinja Alps make their presence felt in three glacial valleys, Matkov kot, Robanov kot and Logarska dolina, and there is also a section of the Karavanke range.

These Slovenian regions boast a wealth of cultural heritage, and the natural environment is magnificent and unspoilt. This Alpine part of Slovenia was mainly a cattle herding area, and known for its typical herder dishes that contained milk and dairy products, along with buckwheat, wheat and maize. Slovenia is known for a number of native breeds, including the Jezersko-Solčavsko sheep, which come from this very area.

The Lower Savinja Valley is in the central part of Slovenia and comprises the valley of the Savinja and its tributaries. Owing to the well-established transport links, a number of important trading routes ran through here (Vienna - Trieste). This area is known for its carting tradition (carrying goods and people on wagons and coaches). From the end of the 15th century these services were an important activity for the local farming people. This region is also characterised by hop-production and a long tradition of brewing.

The Šalek Valley (and the Velenje Basin) is a valley in the north of Slovenia in an area of the north-eastern sub-Alpine foothills. It is bounded in the west by the Kamnik-Savinja Alps, in the east by the Pohorje hills, and in the south by the hills of Posavje. The Paka river runs through Velenje, and the biggest lake is Lake Velenje. Owing to the large number of castles (more than 20), in the Middle Ages the Šalek Valley was known as the 'valley of castles', and this name has stuck to the present day. This place is otherwise most famous for its mining, and at one time there was a thriving sawmilling and timber industry here.

BUCKWHEAT CAKE
AJDNEK

Ajdnek is a precious version of a regular buckwheat cake *potica* with walnuts and honey, which has gained a reputation only in recent decades. It was one of the first desserts prepared in the Upper Savinja Valley, and local custom was to prepare it for All Saints Day, as well as for other important holidays.

Dough:
500 g (1fl 2oz) buckwheat flour
300 g (10oz) wheatflour
7.5 dl (1.25pints) boiling water
Salt

Filling:
500 g (1fl 2oz) ground walnuts
3 dl (10fl oz) honey
5 dl ((16fl oz) lukewarm milk for the topping
Powdered sugar

Preparation:
1. Pour the boiling water over the buckwheat flour, stir, when cooled add wheat flour, yeast and salt.
2. Knead into a fluffy dough.
3. In the meantime, mix the walnuts with lukewarm honey.
4. Pour one third of the dough into a baking pan, sprinkle with the walnuts, and repeat two more layers.
5. The top layer should be the dough, pour the milk over it.
6. Leave to rise for 20 min, pierce gently with a fork several times then bake in the oven at 180° C (350° F) for about 40 min.
7. When done, sprinkle with the powdered sugar.

BOILED BLOOD STUFFING STEW
FIROVŽ

This typical dish, which used to be prepared during the slaughtering season, was almost forgotten. The ingredients that do not keep well had to be used immediately so they enriched the family menu. One such ingredient is pig's blood, which was used to make a special pasta for this soup.

50 g (1.75oz) chops or neck
3 carrots
Fresh parsley
½ celery root
2 cloves garlic
½ onion
Bay leaf, salt, peppercorns, marjoram
1.5 l (2.75 pints) water

Pasta:
2 dl (7fl oz) blood
3 tbsp buckwheat flour
3 tbsp wheat flour
1 tbsp apple cider vinegar

Preparation:
1. Place the meat in cold water, add the seasonings and bring to boil.
2. Add vegetables and cook for 1 hour.
3. In the meantime, mix the pasta ingredients and leave for at least 20 min.
4. Strain the soup, add back the boiled vegetables and deboned meat.
5. Add tiny pasta rolls (*štrukeljci*) and boil for about 10 min.
6. Before serving, soup can be seasoned with 1 tbsp of cider vinegar.

PLUM SOUP
ČEŠPLJEVA JUHA

This regional culinary oddity was usually a part of children's diet – not just because of its sweet taste, but also because it was a quality source of energy, iron and other important nutrients.

500 g (1fl 2oz) plums
2 l (3.5pints) milk
200 g (7oz) hard flour
1 egg
4 tsp sugar
1 tsp salt

Preparation:
1. In a pot, bring the milk to the boil and add salt.
2. Add the plums and sugar, cook for 15 min.
3. Beat the egg, add the flour and make a smooth runny dough.
4. Pour the dough into the soup and cook for 5 min.
5. Leave for 10 – 15 min and mash the ingredients into a coarse consistency.

APPLE - BEAN HOTPOT
JABOLČNI FIŽOL

Apple stew with kidney beans used to be a typical dish throughout the villages of the Slovenian Alps. It can be traced throughout the countryside due to widespread fruit farming and good conditions for growing kidney beans. Each micro region enriched this dish with its distinct mark and specific taste.

250 g (9oz) boiled kidney beans
500 g (1lb 2oz) apples
2 tbsp sugar
1 tbsp lard with cracklings
1 tbsp flour
Cinnamon, ground cloves, salt

Preparation:
1. Peel and slice the apples.
2. In a pan, caramelize the sugar, add the apple slices and some water.
3. Cook for about 15 min, add seasoning and the beans with some water from cooking.
4. Cook for about half an hour, so that the ingredients partially disintegrate.
5. Fry the flour in the lard with cracklings and add to the soup at the end of the cooking.
6. If the soup is too thick, add some water.

SOUR FISH ON BUCKWHEAT PORRIDGE
VLNATA RIBA NA AJDOVI KAŠI

The upper stream of the Savinja River was one of main food sources for the local population. They used a variety of fishing methods as well as efficient techniques of preserving and storing the catch. Fish preserved by brining, smoking, conserved in oil and stored in a multitude of ways were available throughout the year.

1 trout
Bunch of soup vegetables
4 tbsp pumpkin seed oil
3 tbsp vinegar
2 cloves garlic
Salt, black pepper
Buckwheat porridge to accompany the dish

Preparation:
1. Cook the trout in some salted water with the soup vegetables.
2. Remove all bones from the fish and break the fish meat into large pieces.
3. Sprinkle with the pumpkin seed oil and vinegar.
4. Add seasonings and serve on a bed of buckwheat porridge.

Ojstrica.
Photo: Tomo Jeseničnik/www.slovenia.info

KOROŠKA

Although it is one of the smallest regions, Koroška is considered the cradle of the Slovenian nation. Following the plebiscite in 1920 the larger part of Koroška (Carinthia) came under Austrian rule. The Slovenian region of Koroška now encompasses three valleys, the Mežica, the Drava and the Mislinja, which are surrounded by three mountain ranges, the Pohorje, the Karavanke and the Savinja Alps. The unspoilt nature and forests will satisfy the curiosity of any explorer. The magic of Koroška can be found in its precious details created both by humans and nature.

Koroška is associated with charcoal burning, timber rafting and ironworks. The unique creativity of its inhabitants is best observed in folk paintings, woodcarving crafts and special painted beehive panels.

Koroška is rich in forests – dark green spruce forests with an increasing number of larches at higher elevations. It is also a habitat of capercaillies, an endangered bird species.

Slovenj Gradec, Ravne na Koroškem and Dravograd are its biggest towns. Slovenj Gradec is an important business and cultural centre of the region famed for its art galleries and biennial exhibitions of handicrafts. It was also proclaimed a Peace Messenger City by the United Nations.

In the Mežica Valley lies the well-known Ravenska železarna ironworks. In Mežica, the abandoned lead mine has been preserved and converted into an exceptional museum, which is a cultural attraction popular with visitors.

DUMPLINGS WITH DRIED PEARS
KVOČEVI NUDLI

The term 'kvoce' or 'kloce' in the local Koroška dialect denotes dried pears – hence the name kvočevi or kločevi nudlni. 'Nudlni' is a Koroška term for any kind of dough parcel or similar container shaped from dough and stuffed with various fillings or just left empty. This traditional Koroška dish that can be found in the gastronomic strategy, was once a stand-alone treat in combination with a compote. Nowadays it can also feature as a typical local accompaniment to meat.

Parcels:
  500 g flour
  2 eggs
  A little salt
  3 tbsp oil
  2 dl warm water

Filling:
  400 g dried pears
  1 whole egg
  2 dl sour cream
  A handful of breadcrumbs
  Sugar to taste

Preparation:
1. Mix the dough as if for noodle strips, let it sit and roll out thin.
2. Boil the dried pears, allow to cool and chop into small pieces.
3. Mix in the egg, sugar and sour cream and mix until a smooth, thick filling.
4. If the filling is not thick enough, add breadcrumbs.
5. Place the filling three fingers apart on the dough in a line, which you then cover with the other half of the dough.
6. Press your fingers down on the dough between each parcel and expel the air.
7. With a pizza slicer or knife, cut into parcels and start the second row.
8. Boil for 15 minutes in salted water on moderate heat.
9. Garnish with pork rinds or breadcrumbs, or sprinkle with cinnamon and sugar.

LEAVENED PASTRIES
KIPLJENI KNEDLNI

This is another traditional dish from the relatively unknown culinary region of Koroška. It can be served as a stand-alone dish simply to deal with hunger, or later as an accompaniment to various meat or vegetable dishes, in Koroška frequently with soups, and most importantly always with the option of sweet or savoury topping, most popular among which are pork rinds for the savoury-toothed, walnuts and sugar for the sweet-toothed and breadcrumbs for those in-between. 'Kipljeni knedlni', sometimes called just 'kipniki', got their name from 'kipljeno' or risen dough taken from bread dough.

Pastries:
500 g flour
2 eggs
40 g yeast
3 tbsp oil
Milk
Salt

Garnish:
Homemade pork rinds
Breadcrumbs
Butter
Honey or plum jam

Preparation:
1. Mix the leavened dough and shape into a long loaf that should rise again for at least 40 minutes.
2. Boil it wrapped in a cloth, slowly in salted water for 25 minutes on one side and 15 minutes on the other side.
3. Once cooked, slice into circles and garnish with one of the suggested toppings or a combination of them.

COTTAGE CHEESE SPREAD TYPICAL OF KOROŠKA
KOROŠKA SKUTA

At one time pretty much every house in Koroška had a cow, so there were always dairy products to be had. Freshly collected milk was made into cottage cheese and the remainder into various dairy products. This was one of the most typical appetisers in Koroška, and still is today. It involves in fact the preservation of one of the most highly developed crafts in Slovenia – cheesemaking – which at the start of the 19th century had high ambitions to match the level of other European cheese undertakings.

500 g coarse cottage cheese
400 g sour cream
Salt
1 dl pumpkin seed oil
1 onion
Minced pumpkin seeds

Preparation:
1. Mix the cottage cheese, sour cream and salt together well.
2. Mix in a little pumpkin seed oil and shape the mix, placing it in a decorative dish.
3. Pour the rest of the pumpkin seed oil over it, sprinkle roast pumpkin seeds and onion in rings or diced.
4. Add a pinch of caraway seed to taste.

MILLET PORRIDGE WITH FRIED EGG
LUKNJA

A dish with an unusual name – meaning 'hole' in Slovenian – it was once typical of Koroška, but nowadays is more or less unknown. It was named because of the cavity made in the middle of the millet porridge in the pan. It was often eaten to fuel heavy farm work, since it is calorie-rich. Of course it was indispensable when the time came to thresh millet or shuck maize. If this dish was not on the table, the lady of the house would face the discontent of the farmhands, so the young farm lads would try to steal the Luknja or hide it for a while to annoy the others. This dish was also pretty much obligatory for women before or after childbirth.

300 g millet porridge
1 l milk
1 dl sweet cream
Water as needed
Half a tsp salt
1 tsp sugar
250 g butter
4 eggs

Preparation:
1. Cook the millet porridge in salted milk until it softens and thickens.
2. All the while stir it and add milk as needed.
3. Just before it is done, add the sweet cream and sugar, and cook for about another minute.
4. Pour the ready porridge into an appropriate dish and make a cavity or hole in it.
5. Pour melted butter over the porridge.
6. Fry the eggs in the remaining butter then put them in the hole.

BUCKWHEAT STRUDEL BAKED IN CREAM
V SMETANI PEČENI AJDOVI ŠTRUKLJI

What distinguishes this dish is the way the štruklji, a kind of dumpling found almost everywhere in Slovenia, are prepared. Baked in milk or cream is a hallmark of the Koroška heritage, where buckwheat was on the menu every day. Of course this dairy-rich region offered the resources for this kind of dish to evolve. For the most part, buckwheat featured as a gruel in soups or as a mash with potatoes or topped with pork rinds. Otherwise the dish was a part of major church or secular holidays, home celebrations or the end of successful work.

Dough:
  0.5 kg buckwheat flour
  0.5 l salted hot water
  wheat flour for sprinkling

Topping:
  0.7 l sweet cream
  2 tbsp honey

Filling:
  300 g cottage cheese
  3 tbsp sour cream
  2 eggs
  1 tbsp sugar
  3 tbsp honey
  2 tsp breadcrumbs
  Handful of ground walnuts
  Cinnamon

Preparation:
1. Pour the hot salted water over the buckwheat flour, mix and gently knead into a dough.
2. Let stand for 30 minutes.
3. Then roll out the dough on a floured board to the thickness of a knife edge.
4. Mix up the filling from the ingredients and spread over the rolled dough.
5. Sprinkle walnuts over it.
6. Wrap up the dough and cut into parcels about 6 cm long.
7. Place upright one against the other in a greased baking pan.
8. Pour slightly salted sweet cream over them and place in the oven. Bake for at least 45 minutes at 200 degrees.
9. They should soak up all the cream and stay succulent.
10. Drizzle honey over to serve.

Bled Island.
Photo: Branci Ferjan/www.slovenia.info

GORENJSKA

This part of Slovenia has a strong imprint of the Alps and sub-Alpine regions: the two-thousanders of the Julian Alps, which extend in the northwest of Slovenia over the border into Italy, and the peaks of the Karavanke and Kamnik-Savinja Alps. The area of the Slovenian Alps is therefore a meeting point of three major mountain massifs along with the sub-Alpine hills. Triglav is the highest Slovenian peak and a mountain in the Julian Alps, and is also one of the biggest national symbols. Mt Triglav is surrounded by Triglav National Park, an area of 840 square kilometres and one of the most extensive nature reserves in Europe. The Soča and Sava rivers have their sources in Triglav Park, along with the Seven Triglav Lakes and lakes Bohinj and Bled. Lake Bled has an island with a church on it. A special feature of Bled is the 'pletne' boats that serve as 'Bled gondolas'. Gorenjska is one of the most highly developed regions in Slovenia for tourism.

Skiers are drawn to the slopes at Kranjska gora and Krvavec. And Planica is home to a world-famous ski-jump. Thanks to the Alpine herders, Gorenjska has outstanding cheese, and the region is also home to the highly prized kranjska klobasa sausage, which is a protected Slovenian delicacy.

The chief city of the region is Kranj. The main water artery of Gorenjska is the Sava River – the Sava Bohinjka and Sava Dolinka join at Radovljica, birthplace of Slovenian comedy writer Anton Tomaž Linhart. Radovljica is also famous for its Beekeeping Museum. Close to Radovljica is Kropa, an ironworking centre, Železniki, famous for its iron ore, Žiri, famous for its lace, and Brezje, Slovenia's biggest pilgrimage centre. Tržič is famous for its leather crafts.

The delightful village of Vrba at the foothills of the Karavanke is the birthplace of the greatest Slovenian poet, France Prešeren, who wrote Zdravljica (A Toast), which is Slovenia's national anthem.

Another fascinating location is the town of Škofja Loka, famous for its passion play, which was entered in 2008 in the Register of Live Cultural Heritage, and in 2012 the Škofja Loka passion play was declared a living masterpiece of national importance. Since 2016 it has also been on the UNESCO Intangible Cultural Heritage lists.

PANCAKE STRUDEL FROM KRANJ
KRANJSKI ŠTRUKELJ

This variety of rolled and filled pancakes has been on the menu of the "Kot" restaurant since 1936. Today this dish became a part of campaigns led by ethnologists to revive local culinary heritage by adding such dishes to local restaurant menus.

Dough:
   30 dag (10oz) flour
   4 eggs
   1,2 l (2pints) milk
   2 dl (7fl oz) sparkling water
   Salt

Filling:
   50 dag (1fl 2oz) grated pasta dough
   2 eggs
   6 dag (2oz) plain butter
   5 tbsp. of apricot marmalade

Topping:
   2,4 dl (8fl oz) sour cream
   2 eggs

Preparation:
1. Make slightly thicker pancakes.
2. Cook the grated pasta dough in salted water on low temperature, stir while cooking.
3. Leave to cool, mix with the butter, beaten egg and marmalade.
4. Spread the mixture on each pancake, roll and cut into three equal parts, place vertically into a baking dish and cover with the topping.
5. Bake in the oven at 200'C (400'F) for about 10 – 15 min.
6. Serve hot.

CABBAGE STEW
GOVNAČ

Throughout Gorenjska region, this simple food has a variety of names. The name Govnač has its roots in a Slovene word for head, because the dish is made from a whole head of cabbage. It is a simple meal usually made on a workday.

1 head of cabbage
3 potatoes
2 cloves of garlic
3 tbsp. minced lard
2 tbsp. flour
Salt, black pepper

Preparation:
1. Thinly slice the cabbage and boil in salted water for 20 minutes.
2. Peel and dice the potatoes, cook separately.
3. Drain the cabbage and save some water for later.
4. Mash the cooked potatoes, mix with the cabbage and add the seasoning to taste. If consistency is too thick add some water in which the cabbage was cooked.
5. Heat the lard, add the flour and fry briefly, then mix with the cabbage.

BARLEY MUSH WITH PEARS
JEŠPREN S TEPKAMI

This dish was typical for leisure days. Pot barley has been readily available – literally in front of the house. It was dried behind the farmhouse stove and grinded in a local mill. Some of it was used for flour, the rest used mostly for savoury stew named *ričet*. Pot barley enriched with dried or fresh fruit was especially popular.

10 dag (3,5oz) pot barley
Cup of dried pear slices
Handful of prunes
Handful of dried apple slices
1 carrot
Piece of celery root
1 parsley root and leaves
Marjoram, bay leaf, thyme
Black pepper, salt

Preparation:
1. In a pot filled with 2 l of water add the soaked and rinsed pot barley.
2. Add the dried fruits, chopped vegetables and spices.
3. Cook in a covered pot for at least 1 hour.

ŠKOFJA LOKA MILLET MUSH
LOŠKA MEDLA

This simple mushy dish is an ancient meal perfect for feeding a family. At present times it is prepared by prominent chefs from Škofja Loka with variety of side dishes and toppings.

0,5 l (16fl oz) water
5 dag (1,75oz) millet
5 dag (1,75oz) buckwheat or wheat flour
(The picture depicts a fried version)

Preparation:
1. Add the millet into salty boiling water, bring the water to boil again, immediately add the flour and stir.
2. Cook on low temperature, stirring constantly, for about 20 min.
3. Serve warm topped with the pork cracklings, or leave to cool and make small balls.
4. Coat as desired and fry.

DRAŽGOŠE HAND CRAFTED HONEY COOKIES
DRAŽGOŠKI KRUHEK

Originally from Škofja Loka region, the art of making this delicious ornament has been best preserved in Poljanska and Selška valleys. Back in the old days, the purpose of it was for making gifts during religious and other holidays, as a symbol of love, respect and friendship. The design was altered according to specific purpose, yet the most popular forms were heart, circle, half-circle and star. By using two varieties of flour, the makers would achieve a more colourful effect on their hand crafted products.

50 dag (1fl 2oz) honey
1 kg (2,25lb) wheat flour
1 tsp ground cloves
1 tsp ground cinnamon
0,5 dl (16fl oz) water

Preparation:
1. Mix the ingredients into a smooth dough and leave for 30 minutes.
2. Roll the dough 0,5 mm thick, cut out and decorate the ornaments.
3. Bake at 165'C for 10 min.
4. Coat with honey while still warm.
5. If different flours are being used, use one to make the base and another for the ornaments, to achieve a colourful effect.

BOHINJ CREAM PORRIDGE WITH CORN
SMETANČA ALI SMETENJAK Z BOHINJSKO TRDINKO

The easily available reddish corn Trdinka is the main ingredient of this dish, which used to be a staple food of Alpine farmers living in the mountains. They also produced an abundance of dairy products which enhanced the taste and consistency of their dishes.

500 g (1fl 2oz) cornmeal
1 l (1.75pints) fresh cream
Salt
Sugar

Preparation:
1. Bring the cream to the boil, slowly pour in and stir the cornmeal.
2. Cook and stir for 15 - 20 min till thickened, add salt.
3. Pour into a baking dish and leave to cool.
4. Bake in the oven for 15 min at 180° C (350° F) until the crust is golden, or just mash the cold porridge into a bowl.
5. Serve with soured milk or sprinkle with sugar.

Goriška Brda.
Photo: Srdjan Živulović-Bobo/www.slovenia.info

THE SOČA VALLEY, GORIŠKA BRDA, VIPAVA VALLEY

The Soča Valley lies in the northwest of Slovenia and comprises the area along the Soča River, which rises at Trenta in the Julian Alps. The River Soča is a true emerald-coloured gem in the heart of the mountains and a paradise for adventure-seeking visitors, offering white water kayaking, canoeing and rafting. The Soča is also home to the Soča trout, which is an endemic species of Slovenian rivers.

This was also the location of the Soča (Isonzo) Front during the First World War. Ernest Hemingway's novel A Farewell to Arms was set here.

This area was known for its Alpine herding, sheep and goat farming and field crops. The Slovenian poet Simon Gregorčič was born in this area.

Goriška Brda is a borderland area of hills off the beaten track in the far west of Slovenia, and is still mainly a farming region. It is the most Mediterranean part of the Soča Valley, famed for its wine-making and orchards. Although Brda is a small patch of land, it has produced some important people. Brda and Brice were the word associations brought to the world by the poet Alojz Gradnik, who was born in Medana. The biggest attraction of the year is without doubt the festival of cherries at the beginning of June, which is now a traditional event. Grapevines have been cultivated in Brda since the earliest times. The best-known Brda wines are Rebula, Tokay, Pinot, Pinot gris, Chardonnay, Sauvignon, red Merlot and Cabernet.

The Vipava Valley is an area between the high plateaux of Trnovski gozd and Nanos in the north and the Karst plateau in the south. In addition to the city of Nova Gorica, the major settlements of the area include Vipava, Ajdovščina and Solkan. The municipality of Ajdovščina is the economic and cultural centre of the Vipava Valley. A wine road runs through the Vipava Valley.

Visible from afar on a vineyard-covered slope close to Vipava is the renovated Renaissance hunting manor of Zemono, dating back to the 17th century, where once the Counts Lanthieri hosted prodigious parties. Today the Zemono manor house is known mainly as a tourist spot where a popular restaurant serves outstanding cuisine.

CELERY STEW
ŠELINKA

This stew was prepared in the Upper Vipava Valley area during late autumn and winter, because celery keeps well in basements. It was much appreciated during the grape harvesting season, served with potatoes or corn polenta. The recipe has as many varieties as there are households in the village.

1 celery root and leaves
3 potatoes
100 g (3.5oz) prosciutto or bacon
1 carrot
Melissa
Some oil or lard
Salt, black pepper

Preparation:
1. Peel and thinly slice the potatoes, boil and mash with the water from cooking.
2. Dice the prosciutto or bacon and celery, fry together in a pan.
3. After a few minutes, add this mixture and the diced carrots to the mashed potatoes.
4. Add some water (as needed), the chopped celery leaves and season to taste.
5. Cook for about 20 min.

BAKED PASTA
PEČENI BLEKI

Even though pasta was not as popular as polenta in the Vipava area, local housewives used to compete in making interesting designs and toppings for this dish. The pasta making skills and dough originate from neighbouring Italy, the homeland of pasta masters.

250 g (9oz) flour
4 eggs
Topping
Chunks of prosciutto or bacon or cured sausage
Olive oil
Parmesan cheese

Preparation:
1. Make a pliable yet firm dough and leave to sit for about 20 min.
2. Roll into thin sheets and cut into 15 x 15 cm squares.
3. Bake the pasta sheets on a hot stove on both sides, to achieve slightly brownish marks which also add to the distinctive aroma.
4. Break the baked pasta into chunks and toss into boiling salted water, cook for a minute or two and drain.
5. Add the topping made with diced prosciutto or bacon or chopped sausage fried in olive oil. The dish can be sprinkled with some white wine if desired.

DRIED CODFISH WHITE STEW
ŠTOKVIŽ NA BELO

During the times of religious holiday feasting such as Easter and Christmas Eve, this codfish stew was the main dish on the menu. Although codfish originates from the northern seas, it had found its way to this area through merchants from Trieste and had become a local staple food. There are three main recipes for codfish: white stew, red 'goulash' stew and codfish salad.

450 g (1lb) baccala (dried codfish)
10 cloves of garlic
1 tbsp butter
1 tbsp flour
3 dl (10fl oz) milk
Parmesan cheese
Bay leaf
Mixture of olive and plain oil
Salt

Preparation:
1. Soak the baccala overnight, then clean, remove all bones and break the fish meat into small chunks.
2. Save the first water from cooking the fish.
3. Prepare roux from the olive oil, flour, garlic and a chunk of butter.
4. Cover with a lid and cook until thickened, then add the milk and season to taste.
5. Add the parmesan cheese, cook for a few minutes, and briefly dunk the bay leaf to avoid a strong taste.
6. Serve with white polenta and parmesan cheese.

EGG OMELETTE WITH HERBS
FRTALJA

Northern Primorska regional cuisine has always been enriched by a variety of wild and cultivated herbs, which grew in the fields and by the edges of gardens. Eggs were saved for holidays or special occasions, but since the whole region had an abundance of eggs, housewives would sell the eggs or use them to trade for other ingredients. Omelettes have specific micro-location varieties, not just in terms of their specific ingredients but also their thickness. Specific ingredients were determined by nature's offerings during certain periods. If an omelette was desired during winter times, there was usually a chunk of sausage or meat added.

5 eggs
3 tbsp flour
1 dl milk, or more
Handful of feverfew, milfoil and fennel leaves
2 slices of salami
Olive oil
Salt

Preparation:
1. In a large bowl, beat the eggs, add the flour, salt and some milk as needed.
2. Chop the herbs and mix with the olive oil.
3. Fry the egg mixture in the olive oil, turn several times to ensure it is also done on the inside.
4. When done, coat with the herbs soaked in olive oil, serve with the salami.

KOBARID DUMPLINGS
KOBARIŠKI ŠTRUKLJI

This is a variety of pasta pockets, which originate from the Middle Ages, and are a unique culinary peculiarity of this area. It is possible to detect the precise origin of each version by analysing their shape, filling and sometimes the topping. A festive dish with a distinct shape typical of Kobarid that has not evolved for mass production, because the process of making this tasty treat requires lots of skill and precision. It is still on the menu of restaurants dedicated to preserving local culinary traditions.

Dough:
  500 g (1fl 2oz) wheat flour
  4 dl (14fl oz) hot water

Filling:
  300 g (10oz) ground walnuts
  150 g (5.5oz) breadcrumbs
  3 tbsp butter
  Lemon zest
  Handful of raisins
  Rum
  Sugar
  Pinch or cocoa powder

Preparation:
1. Fry the breadcrumbs in the butter, add the walnuts, milk and cocoa.
2. Drain the raisins that have been soaking in rum and add to the breadcrumbs mixture with other ingredients.
3. Mix well into a firm filling.
4. In a large bowl pour over the flour with scalding water and make the dough.
5. Form the filling into a thin roll, cut into pieces and make small balls.
6. Place the filling balls into small sheets of dough, pinch the edges together and in the middle to achieve a typical shape.
7. Cook slowly in hot salted water until the dumplings surface.

COTTAGE CHEESE SOUP
SKUTN'CA

Curd soup was made throughout the year due to the availability of fresh cottage cheese. During colder months, it was enhanced with a smoky taste, which gave it a specific seasonal aroma. Usually served as dinner with some bread or *polenta*, it was made either of cow's, sheep's or goat's milk, and was a staple food for mountain shepherds.

2 dl (7fl oz) water
6 tbsp corn flour
4 tbsp salted cottage cheese
Some herbs, wild growing if available – according to taste.
1 slice of stale bread
Some butter
Salt

Preparation:
1. Slowly pour the corn flour into salted boiling water and mix well to avoid lumps.
2. Add the cottage cheese and season to taste.
3. In a pan fry the bread cut into cubes, add to the soup. Another option is to add some boiled, cooled and grated potatoes.

MUSHED POTATOES WITH VEGETABLE
POŠTOKLJA

Typical for winter and the Primorska region, this dish was named after its preparation method, because the ingredients are mushed (*poštokan*) with a wooden spoon. Dandelion can be replaced with chicory, cabbage or turnip leaves.

4 potatoes
250 g (9oz) dandelion, chicory, or kale leaves
100 g (3.5oz) corn flour
Olive oil
2 cloves of garlic
Salt

Preparation:
1. Peel the potatoes, dice and boil in salted water.
2. Cook the vegetables separately in salted boiling water for 5 min.
3. In a third pan, bring the water to the boil, add salt, olive oil, and slowly pour in the corn flour.
4. Stir constantly and cook for 20 min.
5. Drain the potatoes, mash and mix with the coarsely chopped boiled vegetables.
6. Add the potatoes to the corn mixture and mix together.
7. Season with the garlic fried in olive oil, or with pork cracklings fried in lard.

WHITENED POLENTA WITH COTTAGE CHEESE
OBELJENA POLENTA

This used to be a tasty and energy replenishing meal for shepherds herding their livestock on the mountains. Common polenta, this widely popular side dish that often replaced bread, was enriched with easily available cottage cheese, contributing its refreshing taste and nutritional value.

500 g (1fl 2oz) corn flour
150 g (5.5oz) cottage cheese
3 slices of bacon
2 tbsp smoked cottage cheese
Olive oil
1 dl milk
Pork cracklings
1.5 l (2.25pints) water
Salt

Preparation:
1. Add the corn flour to boiling salted water and stir for about 45 minutes on a low heat.
2. Add the cottage cheese and just briefly mix.
3. Turn over onto a cutting board.
4. Crush the smoked ricotta with a fork and mix with the milk.
5. Fry the finely chopped bacon and cracklings in some olive oil.
6. Place the polenta in a serving dish, top with the warm cracklings and with the cottage cheese leftovers.

Škocjanske jame
Photo: Borut Lozej/www.slovenia.info

NOTRANJSKA, KARST, ISTRIA

The areas of Notranjska and the Karst are characterised by karstic caves, intermittent lakes, gorges and magnificent underground realms. This is home to water, stone, forest, wind and rain. Notranjska was arguably the first region to have become more widely known in the world, thanks to the Slovenian nobleman, castle-owner and polymath Janez Vajkard Valvasor (1641-1693), whose comprehensive opus, The Glory of the Duchy of Carniola, describes the special natural and cultural characteristics of this part of Slovenia.

Notranjska begins with the town of Vrhnika, the birthplace of writer Ivan Cankar. The town also hosts the fascinating Technical Museum of Slovenia. The town of Idrija is notable for its special Idrija-type bobbin lace, one of the finest expressions of Slovenian handicraft traditions. The lace-making school in Idrija was founded in 1876 and is the oldest continually working school of its kind in Europe. The town was also made famous by its mercury mine, now turned into a museum exhibiting many technical inventions and machines.

The region is known too for its numerous Shrovetide Carnival customs, which include Carnival processions in Cerknica and their famous witch. Emerging from the extensive mixed forests of Notranjska, visitors come to a large open karstic polje with the intermittent Lake Cerknica. Together with Rakov Škocjan and Križna jama, the lake has been declared an internationally important wetland – a Ramsar site.

The Karst region (Kras) is famed for its cured ham or prosciutto (kraški pršut). It also gave its name to karstology, the science investigating karst phenomena. Seemingly uninteresting on the surface, the karst underground world is extraordinary and mysterious. Škocjan Caves are a registered UNESCO World Heritage Site. Of all the karstic caves in Slovenia, the most famous is Postojna Cave. It is known not just for its stalactites, stalagmites, baldachins and drapes, but also for the olm or proteus, a cave salamander.

The world-famous white Lipizzaner horses were named after the village of Lipica in the Karst. Some consider these to be the best riding horses in the world.

Slovenian Istria is most strongly associated with the sea. This is a very picturesque and varied landscape, characterised by vineyards, olive trees and Mediterranean fruit trees. On the coast, sea salt and fleur-de-sel are harvested; the sea has fish in abundance; truffles can be found in the woods and meadows. Koper is the biggest coastal city, and is an important harbour and cultural centre. Not far away are the medieval port town of Piran and the modern tourist resort of Portorož. And of course the Sečovlje Salina Nature Park is well worth a visit. It is famous for its traditional method of producing salt, which involves harvesting by hand.

POTATOES IN SAUERKRAUT SOUP
KROMPIR V ZEVNICI

This is a traditional dish from Brkini, or to be more precise, from the Ilirska Bistrica and Pograd area. The ratio between potatoes and sauerkraut was determined by each cook according to their taste and that of their family. Interestingly, potatoes stay firm when cooked with sauerkraut. For this reason some people think that the dish has not been properly cooked, while the locals actually appreciate such texture, which blends well with the softness and freshness of sauerkraut.

1 kg (2.25lb) potatoes
1 kg (2.25lb) sauerkraut
2 tbsp pork lard
150 g (5.5oz) pork chops
1 tbsp cracklings
Piece of smoked bacon
3–4 cloves of garlic
Salt, bay leaf

Preparation:
1. Peel and dice the potatoes, add just enough water to cover.
2. Place the sauerkraut on top, add the seasoning.
3. Cook for at least 30 min, since the potatoes will not overcook due to the sauerkraut.
4. Cut the meat, dice the bacon and fry in lard.
5. Once the potatoes are cooked, drain the water and garnish with the meat.

TURNIP STEW
JOTA Z REPO

Jota is one of those typical staple foods due to the availability of the ingredients even during times of hardship. There are several varieties – with cabbage, with added kidney beans or with potatoes. New versions appeared over time and through different legacies, but the core principle stays the same.

250 g (9oz) pickled turnip
5 potatoes
100 g (3.5oz) cooked kidney beans
Pork lard
Bay leaf, salt
Pork cracklings if desired

Preparation:
1. Boil the pickled turnip in salted water with the seasonings and lard for at least 30 min.
2. Boil the diced potatoes in a separate pot.
3. Mash the potatoes with beans, add the turnip and cook for 15 minutes.
4. Serve with the pork cracklings for a richer taste.

MARINATED FISH
SARDONI NA ŠAVOR

This method of preserving small fish was widespread among fishermen in this area. Created to support survival, it is also a speciality served as a welcome dish by locals.

300 g (10oz) sardines
100 g (3.5oz) flour
Olive oil for frying
4 onions
2 – 3 dl vinegar
Bay leaf, parsley
Salt, black pepper

Preparation:
1. Remove the scales, gut, wash and tap dry the sardines.
2. Roll the sardines in the flour and fry in the olive oil.
3. Add salt after frying.
4. Slice the onions into thin rings and fry or sauté in that same oil.
5. In a large bowl arrange a layer of fish and a layer of onions, repeat layers.
6. Pour over the vinegar.
7. Cover and leave to marinate in a fridge for 2 to 3 days, to develop a full flavour.

PROSCIUTTO SOUP
PRŠUTOVA JUHA

We could name this dish the Post-Easter Soup, since back in the days when a piece of prosciutto might have been worth more than gold, this soup was made only after the prosciutto bone had been cleaned of any edible bits and was ready to be dunked in water.

Prosciutto bone
1 carrot
1 celery stalk
1 onion
Parsley with root and greens
4 l water
Salt and black pepper according to taste

Preparation:
1. Put the prosciutto bone in water, bring to the boil and discard the water (might be too salty – depends on the quantity of meat left over on the bone).
2. Add fresh water and vegetables, boil for about 2 hours.
3. Strain the water, add the chunks of meat and sprinkle with the parsley.
4. Serve with polenta or homemade pasta.

ISTRIAN STRUDEL
ISTRSKI ŠTRUKLJI

The filling was always made one day in advance, to allow a full flavour to develop. This dish was usually made for communion, Easter and other festive occasions, when tables had to be laden with delicacies. In the past, this type of Štruklji dumplings used to be made with filo dough.

Dough:
500 g (1lb 2oz) flour
Sourdough: 1 tsp sugar, 2 tbsp milk, 30 g (1oz) yeast
1 egg
2 dl (7fl oz) milk
1 egg yolk
1 tbsp olive oil
50 g (1.75oz) butter
Some rum
Salt

Topping:
150 g (5.5oz) butter
Breadcrumbs

Filling:
250 g (9oz) ground walnuts
100 g (3.5oz) grated parmesan cheese
1 egg
2 tbsp raisins
2 dl (7fl oz) rum
Breadcrumbs
2 dl (7fl oz) milk
100 g (3.5oz) prosciutto
100 g (3.5oz) cottage cheese
1 tbsp sugar

Preparation:
1. Mix the sourdough starter in a bowl, let rise then add the flour and other ingredients.
2. Add salt and milk as needed.
3. Knead the dough thoroughly and leave to rise for 40 min.
4. Soak the raisins in rum, blanch the walnuts in milk and fry the finely diced prosciutto in oil.
5. Leave to cool and mix with other ingredients.
6. Roll the dough 0.5 cm thick and cover with the filling.
7. Roll the dumpling, place it in a clean kitchen towel and boil in salted water for 45 min.
8. When cooked, cut into thick slices and sprinkle with the breadcrumb topping.

BREAD STUFFING WITH PORK FILLET
NAKL'DA Z OMBOLOM

Nakl'da is a dish that was made during the Easter holidays and is one of the most authentic dishes of the Istria region. It was enjoyed as an appetizer or as a side dish with the main course. The inspiration for creating this dish stemmed from frugality and Easter bread and food leftovers.

Nakl'da
500 g (1fl 2oz) Easter bread
20 g (0.75oz) grated parmesan cheese
4 eggs
Thick slices of bacon or prosciutto
Handful of raisins
Handful of finely chopped summer savory
Olive oil
Salt, black pepper

Ombolo
3–5 medallions of pork fillet (tenderloin)
1 dl (3.5fl oz) olive oil
2 onions
2 dl (7fl oz) red wine (*Refošk*)
Salt, black pepper

Preparation:
1. Crumble the bread leftovers into a large bowl and add the grated cheese.
2. Finely chop the bacon and/or prosciutto and add to the bread mixture.
3. Add all other ingredients and mix.
4. Make about 7 cm long rolls and cook them in salted boiling water.
5. Rub some salt and pepper onto the pork medallions and fry them in a pan with the olive oil.
6. After removing the meat, fry the onions sliced into rings in that same pan.
7. Return the meat to the pan, pour over the red wine and sauté for 20 min.
8. Serve with *Nakl'da*.

Ana Roš
Photo: Hiša Franko Archives

The culinary story of Hiša Franko derives from Slovenian culinary tradition. For our traditional dishes in a new guise – more modern and with new flavours – we use the produce of local farmers, pickers, stockbreeders, beekeepers and herbalists. The Kobarid area, where our restaurant is located, is hidden in one of the most beautiful parts of Slovenia – embraced by mountains, crystal-clear rivers and unspoilt nature. It is from here that I myself also draw inspiration.

When I started cooking I didn't have a lot of knowledge or expertise but I did have a great desire to create the very best from the tradition of the surrounding area and of Slovenian cuisine. I was determined and I also forced myself to learn, so I researched tirelessly and tried a thousand times over to bring individual dishes to the highest level of perfection while retaining their essential and original Slovenian identity. There are many sleepless nights and early mornings behind me, but also a great deal of satisfaction.

I see myself as a Slovenian woman who has chosen to work in haute cuisine. For me, Slovenia is one of the most beautiful countries in the world, with both mountains and the sea. I try to add a personal touch to every dish. I myself have to have a positive or even an emotional connection to it. I still love explaining to diners what there is on the plate we place in front of them in our restaurant.

At Hiša Franko, besides the Slovenian tradition, we also conserve our own family tradition. Our menu still includes the roast beef my husband used to take to school for his lunch. Now, of course, it is presented in a slightly more modern manner. We are also proud of our selection of Slovenian wines. We are an excellent team. Support and cooperation bring the best results.
My message to young chefs is: be sure to appreciate traditional Slovenian cuisine. Present it with pride and interpret it with imagination. I firmly believe that you too can be culinary ambassadors of Slovenia around the world. Your project presents Slovenia as a culinary blend of different geographical areas. And that is why it is wonderful.

I believe that you can help raise Slovenia's profile even further and make it an even more popular culinary destination. Enjoy your cooking and grow as individuals. Persevere and be courageous. Now is the time for Slovenian cuisine! We already have everything – nature's gifts and tradition. All we need to do is write a wonderful story with it. With everything we take from the environment where we have grown up, we write a new chapter in its history. Let this history also include your story. The fact that you prize and value Slovenia's culinary tradition just as I do fills me with enthusiasm.

It is famous for its traditional method of producing salt, which involves harvesting by hand.

Ana Roš, Hiša Franko
World's Best Female Chef 2017

KUHNAPATO.SI

GRANDMA'S KITCHEN, Recipes from Slovenia

Publisher	Government Communication Office of the Republic of Slovenia
Director	Kristina Plavšak Krajnc, M.Sc.
Head of State Promotion Section	Petra Ložar
Editors	Anka Peljhan and Polona Prešeren, M.Sc.
Text about regions	Tanja Glogovčan
Design	Irena Kogoj
Photo Editor	Foto format d.o.o.
Photos	Igor Zaplatil and Ljubo Vukelić, Delo d.d.
Photo on the front page	Matevž Kostanjšek and Gruša Zorn/www.slovenia.info
Translation	Secretariat-General of the Government of the Republic of Slovenia, Translation and Interpretation Division, DZTPS, Amidas
Language editing	Amidas
Print	Collegium Graphicum d.o.o.
Number of copies	3000

3rd reprint
Ljubljana, April 2019

Project Kuhnapato is supported by Ministry of Health; Ministry of Agriculture, Forestry and Food; Ministry of Education, Science and Sport; and Government Communication Office of the Republic of Slovenia.

Honorary Patron of the Project Kuhnapato is Dr Miro Cerar, Prime Minister of the Republic of Slovenia.